Metro-Goldwyn-M

AND

CINERAMA

PRESENT

HOW THE
WEST
WAS WON

A RANDOM HOUSE BOOK

They came by the thousands from everywhere, for to them the West was the promise of the future.

HOW THE WEST WAS WON

1839-1889

"...moving yet and never stopping,
Pioneers! O Pioneers!"

WALT WHITMAN

HURON DISTRICT

DISTRICT

NEW YORK

MASS.

CONN.

R.I.

MAINE

N.H.

N.J.

DEL.

MD.

OHIO

VIRGINIA

CAROLINA

KANSAW TERRITORY

GEORGIA

FLORIDA

UNITED STATES.

Scale

50 100   200   300   500   600 Miles

THE MGM CINERAMA STORY

★ ★ ★ ★ ★ ★ ★ ★ ★ ★ ★ ★ ★ ★ ★ ★ ★ ★ ★ ★

THE conquest of the American West has lived as one of the great adventures of history. Immortalized in story, song and legend, it has never ceased to stir man's imagination.

The American pioneer was lured by the great unknown. Dauntless, courageous, and defiant of risk, he was as heroic in his era as today's astronaut. The pioneer's constant companions were hardship and danger—from Indians on the warpath to stampeding buffalo herds. Across 2500 miles, each step Westward led to disaster and death; but the West also held the promise of good fortune and handsome reward if he could survive the hardships.

The land the pioneer sought to win was a stubborn and unrelenting enemy. Mighty rivers filled with the fury of white-water rapids, endless plains of parched earth, mountains like forbidden granite fortresses barred his Westward trek. None of these halted the pioneer, as he pushed toward the West doggedly beyond each day's setting sun.

The winning of the American West is a story of infinite excitement. It is a story that requires telling on the screen, but only on a screen with dimensions to match its breadth.

Metro-Goldwyn-Mayer and Cinerama decided to produce dramatic story films in the magnificent Cinerama medium. The creative power of the world's largest motion picture facilities and the unique Cinerama process established a collaboration big enough to capture the story of the West.

When the MGM-Cinerama agreement was reached by Joseph R. Vogel, President of MGM and Nicolas Reisini, President and Chairman of the Board of Cinerama Inc., Cinerama was soon on the move to Hollywood. Fleets of trucks moved the company's headquarters from Oyster Bay, N. Y., to the MGM Studios in California. The nearby Forum Theatre was redesigned as research center for the multimillion dollar Cinerama cameras and special equipment. Former Cinerama techniques were improved and new and better ones were developed to prepare for filming the epic of the West.

The story of the American West is many-faceted. What was needed next was a text which could capture its most dynamic aspects—a story that could bring the thrill of authenticity to the large participating audience. The basis for such a story was published in *Life* magazine as seven articles on the American West. It was a publishing sensation when it appeared, and was read by about 25,000,000 people.

This dramatic series inspired HOW THE WEST WAS WON. It encompassed all the most important highlights of the winning of the West, and provided a subject suitable to the size and scope of Cinerama. As mighty action flows across the screen everyone can affirm that Cinerama tells a story more brilliantly, more colorfully and more dynamically than any other contemporary medium.

Today's magnificent Cinerama system is as different from the original Cinerama created by the late Fred Waller as today's jet airplanes differ from the first simple airplanes.

What is Cinerama? In the beginning, it was a man's dream. Both genius and practical scientist, Waller sought in the mid-30s to create the illusion of reality on the screen. Years of trial and error brought Waller to his goal—three cameras mounted as one, with a single shutter. Three 27 mm lenses of these cameras covered a field 146 degrees wide by 55 degrees high, approximating the scope of the human eye, the most perfect of all lenses.

The range of this three camera set up is ideal for projecting an image that can be viewed in full dimension by an audience in a theatre. The result is a gigantic image that figuratively wraps the world around a theatre seat and its occupant.

Cinema-Sound, a seven track, seven channel system of almost perfect fidelity, was added to the three camera system. This made it possible to follow the action moving across the vast

A lone buffalo hunter stalks a herd of the majestic animals which 100 years ago were estimated to number 60,000,000.

screen not only with the eyes but with the ears and the emotions as well.

Collaboration between technicians of Cinerama and Metro-Goldwyn-Mayer has produced improved cameras, lenses, screens, transistorized sound, sharper production and printing. Continued technical refinements for "story-telling" films, has given Cinerama new reality of photography and sound. The Cinerama technical staff, headed by Thomas Conroy. Vice President in Charge of Production, also includes camera consultant Walter Gibbons-Fly, Cinerama sound consultants, Fred Bosch and Ray Sharples. The Metro-Goldwyn-Mayer technical staff is one of the largest and most respected in the film industry.

In HOW THE WEST WAS WON, Cinerama audiences will see and hear more than ever before in a film so great in scope that it could only have been produced in Cinerama. To assure a constant flow of great entertainments in Cinerama, Metro-Goldwyn-Mayer and Cinerama simultaneously filmed George Pal's wonder filled production of THE WONDERFUL WORLD OF THE BROTHERS GRIMM.

These two motion pictures in Cinerama are indeed monumental entertainments of tomorrow brought to great audiences today!

A tiny pioneer raft gamely tackles the roaring rapids of the Ohio, gateway river to the West.

THE STARS

CARROLL BAKER:
Eve Prescott, pioneer wife and
mother. A product of the famed
Actors Studio, Miss Baker was born
in Johnstown, Pa., and began her
career in television commercials.
Discovered by Elia Kazan, she appeared on the stage in "All Summer
Long" and became an overnight film
star in Kazan's "Baby Doll." She has
since appeared in numerous important films.

KARL MALDEN:
Zebulon Prescott, a sod buster. This
actor's distinguished career began on
Broadway in Maxwell Anderson's
"Truckline Cafe." The first film to
bring him to public attention was
Tennessee Williams' "A Streetcar
Named Desire," in which he won
an Academy Award as best support-
ing actor. He also has achieved success as a director, and his other films
include "Ruby Gentry" and "On
the Waterfront." He was born in
Gary, Indiana.

LEE J. COBB:

Lew Ramsay, a frontier marshal. Recognized internationally as an actor of unusual versatility, Cobb was born in New York and studied to be an aeronautical engineer before deciding to become an actor. Years of struggle preceded his first success on the Broadway stage in "Clash by Night." Other plays have included "Jason," "Golden Boy" and "Death of a Salesman." His film credits include "Anna and the King of Siam" and "On the Waterfront."

HENRY FONDA:

Jethro Stuart, buffalo hunter. At home on stage, screen and in television, Nebraska-born Fonda began his acting career with a playhouse in Omaha after studying journalism at the University of Minnesota. He served with the Navy in the Pacific during World War II. His stage credits include "Mister Roberts" and "The Caine Mutiny Court-Martial." His films include "Ox-Bow Incident," "Mister Roberts" and "War and Peace."

CAROLYN JONES:

Julie, wife of a frontier lawman. Born in Amarillo, Texas, Miss Jones has established herself as a star of motion pictures, stage and television. For HOW THE WEST WAS WON, she forgoes her usual youthful, romantic roles to portray a middle-aged frontier wife. Her film credits include "The Tender Trap," "A Hole in the Head" and "Bachelor Party."

GREGORY PECK:

Cleve van Valen, tinhorn gambler. This actor has the distinction of having been starred in every one of his motion pictures. Born in La Jolla, California, he returned to the West Coast after a career on Broadway. His film credits include "Spellbound," "Gentlemen's Agreement," "The Paradine Case," "Roman Holiday," "The Snows of Kilimanjaro" and "Pork Chop Hill," which he also produced.

GEORGE PEPPARD:

Zeb Rawlings, soldier-turned-lawman. Born in Detroit, Michigan, this ex-Marine is a graduate of Purdue University. After his stage debut in 1949 at the Pittsburgh Playhouse, he enrolled in the Actors Studio in New York and worked in summer stock. An appearance in "The Pleasure of His Company" on Broadway led to an MGM contract and his debut in "Home From the Hill." He also starred with distinction in "Breakfast at Tiffany's."

ROBERT PRESTON:

Roger Morgan, wagonmaster. Robert Preston was born in Newton Highlands, Mass. After attending school in Los Angeles, he joined the Pasadena Community Playhouse. Forty-two plays later, he was signed by Paramount and became a star in "Union Pacific." After starring in such films as "Beau Geste," "Reap the Wild Wind" and "Northwest Mounted Police," he returned to the stage as star of "The Music Man," a role he has re-created for the screen.

DEBBIE REYNOLDS:

Lillith Prescott, gambler's bride. Born in El Paso, Texas, but raised in Hollywood, Debbie Reynolds won the Miss Burbank contest and an MGM contract at the same time. Her boop-boop-a-doop performance in "Three Little Words" led to a career which has included dozens of important motion pictures, among them "Singin' in the Rain," "Tammy and the Bachelor," "The Catered Affair," "Susan Slept Here" and "The Tender Trap."

JAMES STEWART:

Linus Rawlings, mountain man. Stewart was born in Indiana, Pa., and joined the Falmouth Players after graduation from Princeton University. He was decorated for his service in the Air Force in World War II and is a Brigadier General in the Air Force Reserve. His films have included "The Philadelphia Story," for which he won the Academy Award, "The Glenn Miller Story," and "Anatomy of a Murder."

SPENCER TRACY:

The Narrator. Although this famous star, one of the few ever to be honored by two Academy Awards, does not appear in the film, his magnificent speaking voice has the important role of narrating the stirring drama of the winning of the West. His Oscars came for "Captains Courageous" and "Boys' Town," and this Milwaukee-born star also has appeared in "Boom Town," "Northwest Territory," "Thirty Seconds Over Tokyo," "Bad Day at Black Rock" and "Judgment at Nuremberg."

ELI WALLACH:

Charley Gant, outlaw leader. Another product of New York's Actors Studio, Wallach was born in New York, and now divides his time between stage and screen, plus an occasional television performance. Among his stage hits have been "The Cold Wind and the Warm," "Camino Real," "Teahouse of the August Moon." His film credits include "The Magnificent Seven," in which he won international acclaim portraying a Mexican bandit.

JOHN WAYNE:

General Sherman at Shiloh. One of filmdom's outstanding outdoor actors, Wayne was born in Winterset, Iowa, attended school in California and played varsity football at the University of Southern California. He now is both star and producer. Among his ninety motion pictures, including some of the most successful ever made, are "The Quiet Man," "Stagecoach," "The Horse Soldiers," "She Wore A Yellow Ribbon," "Red River" and "The Alamo."

RICHARD WIDMARK:

Mike King, empire builder. After a brief career as a teacher, Widmark entered the theatre and appeared in such hits as "Kiss Me Kate"; but it was the motion picture, "Kiss of Death," which gave him an international reputation. Born in Sunrise, Minnesota, and educated at Lake Forest University in Illinois, his major roles have included "Panic in the Streets," "Broken Lance," "Prize of Gold," "Saint Joan" and "Time Limit."

THE CO-STARS

BRIGID BAZLEN, born in Fond du Lac, Wisconsin, portrays Dora Hawkins, the cunning temptress daughter of a renegade river pirate preying on unsuspecting pioneer families.

WALTER BRENNAN, born in Lynn, Massachusetts, and three-time Oscar winner, creates Colonel Hawkins, a river pirate, who matches wits with a mountain man and loses.

DAVID BRIAN, born in New York City, portrays the Van Valen family attorney who must console an aging widow while her possessions are sold at auction.

ANDY DEVINE, born in Flagstaff, Arizona, plays Corporal Petersen, the simple postman who finds glory in a gaudy Union uniform during the Civil War.

RAYMOND MASSEY, born in Toronto, Canada, and television's famed Doctor Gillespie, recreates his memorable characterization of "Abe Lincoln in Illinois."

AGNES MOOREHEAD, born in Boston, Massachusetts, portrays Rebecca Prescott, courageous farmer's wife, who follows her husband into the unknown wilderness.

HENRY (Harry) MORGAN, born in Detroit, Michigan, plays the indomitable General Ulysses S. Grant, who changed the course of American history at the Battle of Shiloh.

THELMA RITTER, born in Brooklyn, New York, portrays Agatha Clegg, plainswoman in search of a new land and a man, any man who comes along.

MICKEY SHAUGHNESSY, born in New York City, and a noted night club comedian, plays a straight role as a deputy marshal in a lawless Arizona mining town.

RUSS TAMBLYN, born in Los Angeles, California, plays a young Confederate soldier from Texas who, like many a Union soldier, wasn't quite sure what he was fighting for.

"...**T**he West was won by the pioneer. He blazed trails, gutted mountains, ran furrows, and planted corn on the prairies..."

WILLIAM MacLEOD RAINE: *Guns of the Frontier*

The mountain man Linus comes down out of the high country with a rich haul of pelts and greets friendly Indians at their camp.

River pirate Hawkins uses deceitful daughter as lure in attempt to steal Linus' rich haul of beaver pelts.

The Erie Canal was the great jumping off point for those heading into the vast unknown land to the West.

Linus and Eve fall in love the first time they meet each other in the Ohio Valley.

The Prescotts battle valiantly to save their raft when it gets caught in the swirling rapids of the mighty river.

"**T**hrough the battle, through defeat
Moving yet and never stopping
Pioneers! Oh Pioneers!"

WALT WHITMAN: *Pioneers! Oh Pioneers!*

Through the vast and beautiful land the pioneer pushed civilization ever westward.

Feeling the white men to be usurpers in their land, the Indians attacked wagon trains with ferocious frequency.

Romance on the frontier was fast and to the point as Lilith and Cleve discover love.

Cleve, the gambler, is quick to put his money into any game of chance.

Indians show little mercy as they attack a wagon train moving across their domain.

Lillith skillfully uses a bullwhip to convince Morgan she is rugged enough for the frontier.

As civilization came to the West the demand for entertainment increased.

General Sherman tries to convince a discouraged General Grant he must not resign as Commander.

"**N**ow we are engaged in a great civil war, testing whether that nation, or any nation so conceived and so dedicated, can long endure."

ABRAHAM LINCOLN: *Gettysburg Address*

Eve realizes she cannot prevent Zeb from going to war, and bravely gives him her permission to join the Union Army.

Union troops advance under fire at Battle of Shiloh.

Zeb and Reb, on different sides, meet as lost humans seeking reason for war and destruction.

"**A** million buffalo is a great many, but I am certain that I saw that many yesterday."

HORACE GREELEY, 1859

Laborers lay track for railroad to open door to West.

Men leap for their lives as the water tower is tumbled by onrushing buffalo herd.

Jethro, the buffalo hunter, whose job is to provide food for the railroad builders.

A mighty sea of destruction as buffalo herd rampages through railroad construction camp.

Zeb and Jethro promise warlike Arapahoes their hunting grounds will remain unmolested.

Mike, the empire build-
er, and Zeb stand side
by side against onslaught
by the attacking Indians.

At saloon, Mike refuses
to believe Zeb's predic-
tions of an Indian attack.

Raging gun battle occurs when bandits encounter the law.

"...those who break the great law
of Heaven by shedding man's blood
seldom succeed in avoiding discovery."

DANIEL WEBSTER

Train carrying shipment of gold breaks apart after bandit attack.

A moment of extreme danger...

Charley Gant and band of outlaws are ready for blazing gun battle.

Marshal Lou Ramsey and deputy join together to await expected ambush.

Lilith informs her attorney that she will move to Arizona.

A MONUMENTAL PRODUCTION

★ ★ ★ ★ ★ ★ ★ ★ ★ ★ ★ ★ ★ ★ ★ ★ ★ ★ ★ ★

FILMING the fully definitive story of the winning of the American West was one of the most demanding projects ever undertaken. This was never attempted before.

The story encompasses fifty years in the westward expansion of the American nation—from 1839 to 1889. It includes momentous historic events of that era related to the personal stories of three generations of a typical pioneer family.

Long before this heroic drama was placed before the Cinerama cameras, the project demanded and utilized the vast resources of Metro-Goldwyn-Mayer, the world's largest studios, and the Cinerama Corporation.

Before filming, the collaboration took four directions—historical research, scientific research to refine and improve Cinerama techniques, production planning, including script writing and casting, and selection of locations for shooting.

Bernard Smith received the assignment of producer, and it was he who guided the four aspects. James R. Webb, noted writer and authority on the history of America, won the assignment of writing the original screenplay.

Metro-Goldwyn-Mayer and Cinerama united to meet the challenge of filming a full-length drama in the remarkable Cinerama medium—a challenge that tested the ingenuity of artists and artisans and the full resources of both corporations.

Every phase of production was geared to the remarkable capacity of the Cinerama camera to capture for the screen a motion picture with absolute reality. HOW THE WEST WAS WON concerns itself with the rich human stories of our pioneers.

The search for locations for the filming was one of the most extensive ever inaugurated by a film company. Over 75 per cent of the film was filmed on locations far from the studios in Culver City, Califor-

At historic Smithland, Kentucky, oldest town on the Ohio River, cast and crew assemble for the trip to a location miles away.

Director Henry Hathaway (back to camera) and Cinerama's Tom Conroy (peering through lens) plan an Erie Canal scene setup.

Stewart, a talented musician, entertains Miss Baker and Miss Reynolds on the accordion, between scenes in Illinois.

nia. Each locale had to be devoid of any signs of civilization.

The entire Metro-Goldwyn-Mayer staff of location experts searched for locations which would recall the America of the 1800s. These men traveled through the historic Ohio River Valley, once a water highway to the West, and into the heart of the proud Rocky Mountains. They rode over unused paths and roads as long as four-wheeled vehicles would carry them, and by foot along trails where there were no roads. They took thousands of photographs and sent them back to the studio as often as they could get to a post office. From these efforts came eleven key locations.

Among the locations selected were the Black Hills of South Dakota, sacred land of the Sioux Indians, and home of the largest remaining herd of buffalo in the United States; the Uncompaghre National Forest in the Rockies of Colorado which has an average elevation of 11,500 feet and where there are 52 peaks towering above 14,000 feet. In addition, the area bordering the Ohio and Cumberland Rivers in Kentucky were selected, where pioneers had sailed rafts and mountain men had paddled their pelt-laden canoes. Monument Valley on the Arizona-Utah border, one of nature's spectacular wonders also was an

Miss Reynolds brought safely ashore after being tossed into the ice cold Gunnison River in Colorado. Director Hathaway (back to camera) supervising the action.

Behind-the-camera view of the hazardous wagon train river crossing 11,000 feet in the Rocky Mountains.

important location.

The production brought together Hollywood's most experienced creators, craftsmen and technicians, utilizing each of thirty-eight specialized MGM departments representing 117 arts and professions and 253 skilled technical crafts.

The screenplay focused on five closely related yet distinct periods—the early days of the Ohio River Valley, the covered wagon and gold rush, the Civil War, the building of the transcontinental railroad and the Southwest. With the most careful scheduling, the film could not conceivably be completed in less than ten months. If one director and cinematographer were to have carried the entire burden, it would have required years to complete the motion picture.

To solve the problem of time, three of Hollywood's most renowned directors and four veteran camera-

men worked closely and combined their special talents. The directors were John Ford, Henry Hathaway and George Marshall, and the cinematographers were William Daniels, Milton Krasner, Charles Lang, Jr., and Joseph La Shelle. These men were vastly stimulated by the storytelling potential of Cinerama and they adapted themselves to this new medium. They made many contributions to the art and craft of Cinerama to provide more exciting dramatic action.

This was equally true of everyone connected with HOW THE WEST WAS WON. Hollywood's unusual interest in the picture made it possible to assemble the splendid cast starring Carroll Baker, Lee J. Cobb, Henry Fonda, Carolyn Jones, Karl Malden, Gregory Peck, George Peppard, Robert Preston, Debbie Reynolds, James Stewart, Eli Wallach, John Wayne,

Director John Ford rehearses a scene with Eve and Zeb.

PRODUCTION NOTES

It required more than two months for wranglers to corral the 2000 buffalo seen in the film's spectacular stampede scene, filmed in South Dakota.

★ ★ ★

More than 5000 pairs of period shoes and Indian moccasins were hand made to be worn by characters in HOW THE WEST WAS WON.

★ ★ ★

Thousands of yards of homespun material had to be ordered from ancient looms in India for the special costumes. The Cinerama

cameras are so critical they show up as false any attempts to substitute modern fabrics with machine stitching. So, all costumes had to be sewn by hand.

★ ★ ★

Five famous Indian tribes are represented among the Indian personnel of the film—the Brules, Oclallas and Minnecanjous of the Sioux nation, and the Arapahoes and Cheyennes.

★ ★ ★

Among the real Indians in the film are 81 year old Chief Weasel of the Oglalla tribe, a survivor of

the Wounded Knee Massacre, who spent eight years with the Buffalo Bill Cody Show; and Red Cloud, who helped wipe out Custer's forces at the Little Big Horn; and Ben Black Elk, son of a medicine man and the most photographed Indian in America today.

★ ★ ★

Twenty thousand pounds of hay and 1000 pounds of grain were needed daily to feed the 600 horses used in the production. Thousands more pounds of feed were needed for buffalo and other stock used in the film.

The 850 pound triple lensed Cinerama camera focuses on the railroad building scene in South Dakota.

Richard Widmark and co-starring Brigid Bazlen, Walter Brennan, David Brian, Andy Devine, Raymond Massey, Agnes Moorehead, Henry (Harry) Morgan, Thelma Ritter, Mickey Shaughnessy and Russ Tamblyn. Spencer Tracy became the twenty-fourth star of the cast, and although he is not seen in the picture, he serves in the vital role of narrator. His rich and dramatic voice weaves together the threads of history's tapestry as the West is won.

In total, a year of meticulous preparation was spent preceding the actual start of camera work.

The research alone filled 87 volumes which were cross indexed for easier reference. These included more than 10,000 photographs, paintings and sketches which became the source of authentic background information. It was a library for the directors, the set designers, the costumers, the makeup and hairdressing craftsmen. The material provided information on how the pioneer built his crude rafts, his tools and cooking equipment, and the types of weapons he and his Indian adversaries used. The Metro-Goldwyn-Mayer research department purchased 195 books which were added to an already outstanding collection of early Americana.

A steady stream of color drawings and sketches came from the studio's art department. Visualizations depicting all of the action from river crossing by covered wagons to Indian battles were made. Seventy-seven individual sets were designed. Sets were built higher, wider and more complete than before because

Debbie Reynolds, Gregory Peck and Thelma Ritter in a behind-the-scenes moment during production.

The Cinerama camera captures the grandeur of California's Sierra Nevada Mountains in epic scene.

Director George Marshall outlines a scene for Henry Fonda and Richard Widmark.

the Cinerama camera magnifies each detail tremendously.

Closeups of Debbie Reynolds, or of Gregory Peck, were filmed at two or three feet, and in pre-production tests, it was discovered that the camera glaringly revealed such minute things as machine stitching on the costumes. So, each garment had to be remade and sewn by hand in the studio's wardrobe department.

There could be no substitute for the rough, uneven homespun materials worn by the pioneers. Fifty yards of any particular fabric was the minimum order accepted by the few factories still specializing in these fabrics. A major source, oddly enough, was India, where the ancient art of handlooming has survived a mechanical age. Thousands of yards of this homespun were purchased for the costume department.

All the moccasins available in stores on Indian reservations around the nation were purchased for the production, but even these were not enough to supply the 1500 pairs used in this picture. Still more were handmade by Indian craftsmen on special order, and studio bootmakers turned out 2300 pairs of period shoes. Indian craftsmen made authentic headdresses, mostly of genuine eagle feathers and hundreds of yards of intricate beadwork.

John Wayne and Director John Ford, long time friends and co-workers, discuss a scene together.

Henry Fonda chats with two members of the Arapahoe tribe while on location in the Black Hills of South Dakota.

The total number of wardrobe items ran into multiple thousands. It was the most exacting costume assignment ever attempted for a motion picture.

A few production statistics, selected at random, give a general idea of the problems faced. Bit players and extras appearing in the film totaled 12,617. There were 630 horses, 150 mules and 50 head of oxen which were tended by 203 wranglers. From reservations in South Dakota, Colorado and Utah, 350 Indians were recruited. There were 107 Conestoga and trail wagons.

Paradoxically, without modern transportation, it would have been impossible for the film crew to follow the trail of the pioneers across America. No mass movement in the history of filming on location comes close to matching HOW THE WEST WAS WON. The entire company was literally placed on wheels. It was completely self-contained, from portable dressing rooms for the stars to compact 7500 pound Leroi generators to furnish the millions of candlepower needed to light the various sets and locations.

At the height of production, the pool of studio vehicles, continually on the move over transcontinental highways for months on end, numbered 71, including 55 foot, 18 wheel semi-trailer trucks with 60,000 pound capacity, 50 foot vans, two-ton vans, four wheel drive equipment, caterpillars, buses, station wagons and passenger cars.

From the start of production on May 26, 1961, in the Ohio River Valley, with headquarters at Paducah, Kentucky, this group of vehicles accumulated almost a million miles of travel while shuttling between the studio and locations all over America.

Many of the locations selected for the film had never been photographed for a motion picture. Battery Rock in the Ohio River Valley, Courthouse Mountain, the Pinnacles and Chimney Rock in the Colorado Rockies were such areas. Locations were established in the high Sierras, the hills and plains of South Dakota and arid stretches of desert in the Southwest. To reach some of the more inaccessible locations, it was often necessary to bulldoze and maintain roads to accommodate the massive equipment needed at the sites. As the last vestiges of the Old West rapidly disappear, HOW THE WEST WAS WON recaptures both the stories and the land of the pioneers.

The spirit of the Old West is relived in the songs it inspired. The tunes, tender and haunting, love ballads, and stirring marches which came from the hearts of the pioneers, have been woven into the score of HOW THE WEST WAS WON.

Heading a team of outstanding musical talent is Alfred Newman, an Academy Award winner five times. He won his first Oscar for "Alexander's Ragtime Band" and subsequently for "Song of Bernadette," "Mother Wore Tights," "Love Is A Many Splendored Thing" and "The King and I."

Associated with Newman are: Robert Emmett Dolan, music co-ordinator; Ken Darby, who wrote the lyrics to the film's title song, with music by Newman; and Sammy Cahn, Academy Award winner in collaboration for the song "Three Coins In The Fountain." Mr. Cahn wrote the lyrics for "Home In The Meadow," recurring theme of HOW THE WEST WAS WON.

Newman's score includes authentic songs of each historical period — the Rivers, the Plains, the Civil War, the Railroad and the Outlaws. His overture contains songs which will live as long as there is an America, among them "Shenandoah," and "Bound For the Promised Land."

In every aspect, HOW THE WEST WAS WON was a memorable project. The end result presents for the first time on a screen vast enough to capture its scope, the titanic story of the winning of the West.

* * * * * * * * * * * * * * * * * * *

THE PRODUCER

BERNARD SMITH unknowingly devoted most of his life preparing to produce HOW THE WEST WAS WON. Born in New York and educated at Columbia University, he was an editor at Alfred A. Knopf Inc. from 1929 until 1944. During that period, he rose to editor in chief and frequently edited books on American history and the American West. In 1946 he became story editor for Samuel Goldwyn, and later served in various executive positions with Paramount, Edward Small Productions, and Hecht-Hill-Lancaster. He produced his first film, "Elmer Gantry," in 1960. HOW THE WEST WAS WON is the first he has produced since joining MGM in 1960.

THE WRITER

JAMES R. WEBB has earned an outstanding reputation as a writer. Born in Denver and educated at Stanford University, he began writing fiction in 1936 and screenplays in 1938, and his work has appeared in almost every American magazine of importance. During World War II he served with distinction in North Africa and Europe. Since 1951 he has written screenplays exclusively, and among his successful credits are "The Big Country," "Trapeze" and "Pork Chop Hill."

THE CINEMATOGRAPHERS

WILLIAM DANIELS, A.S.C., born in Cleveland, Ohio, gave up the study of law at the University of Southern California to join the motion picture industry as a cinematographer. He was first an assistant cameraman at Triangle Studios in 1917 and became a first cameraman the following year at Universal. Daniels moved to the newly formed Metro-Goldwyn-Mayer in 1924 and photographed most of the films starring the glamorous Greta Garbo. He won an Academy Award in 1948 for "Naked City."

MILTON KRASNER, A.S.C., began his career as an assistant cameraman and camera operator in 1918 at the old Vitagraph and Biograph Studios in New York City where he was born. He became a first cameraman in 1927, and Academy Award winner in 1954 for his photography of "Three Coins in the Fountain." He photographed "Double Life," which won an Academy Award for Ronald Colman, and "Farmer's Daughter," the film for which Loretta Young received her Oscar. He also was cinematographer on the Academy Award winning "All About Eve."

CHARLES BRYANT LANG, JR., A.S.C., like Daniels, was a law student at the University of Southern California when he also became interested in the art of photography. Starting in the Paramount Film Laboratories he came to the attention of Cameraman H. Kinley Martin who made him his assistant. He soon advanced to the position of Cinematographer and won an Academy Award in 1933 for his photography of "Farewell to Arms," and has been nominated three times since for "Queen Bee," "Separate Tables" and "Some Like It Hot."

JOSEPH LaSHELLE, A.S.C., was set for a career as an Electrical Engineer until he took a summer job in the old Lasky Laboratory. This was so fascinating he remained and soon became superintendent of the printing room at the Paramount Laboratory. In 1925, Cameraman Charles K. Clark chose him as his assistant. "The Happy Land" was LaShelle's first assignment as a Cinematographer. This was followed by a group of outstanding films among them "Laura," which brought him an Academy Award in 1944. Since then he has had three Award nominations for "Marty," "Career" and "The Apartment."

THE DIRECTORS

HENRY HATHAWAY, born in Sacramento, California, is acknowledged as one of the industry's foremost directors of fast moving, action films. He began his remarkable career at the age of eight as a child actor. Hathaway first commanded critical attention for his work on "Lives of the Bengal Lancers." Since that time has delivered an imposing list of outstanding productions, among them "The Trail of the Lonesome Pine," which was the first outdoor film photographed in color. Among his other hits are such motion pictures as "Peter Ibbetson," "Go West, Young Man," "Souls at Sea," "Spawn of the North," "Brigham Young" and "North to Alaska." For HOW THE WEST WAS WON he directed the sequences on the rivers, the plains and the outlaws.

JOHN FORD is Hollywood's only four time Academy Award-winning director. He received Oscars for "The Informer" (1935), "Grapes of Wrath" (1940), "How Green Was My Valley" (1941) and "The Quiet Man" (1952). Ford, born in Cape Elizabeth, Maine, was given his first directorial assignment in 1917, the film being a two reel Western. Since that time he has directed such all time greats as "The Iron Horse," "Arrowsmith," "Stagecoach," "She Wore a Yellow Ribbon" and "Mr. Roberts," to mention only a few. During World War II he served as Lieutenant Commander with the U.S. Navy in the Pacific and European theatres. He achieved the rank of Rear Admiral. For HOW THE WEST WAS WON he directed The Civil War sequence.

GEORGE MARSHALL, born and educated in Chicago, Illinois, has directed more than four hundred feature motion pictures during a career spanning a half century. He literally was trained in every phase of movie making. He joined the old Universal Studios in 1912 and was successively an extra, bit player, prop boy, makeup man, film editor, cameraman, casting director and assistant director. He directed his first film, a three reel Western, in 1913. During his early career Marshall directed such stars as Ruth Roland, Lloyd Hamilton and Tom Mix. He saw service in World War I, and his films have included "Destry Rides Again," "Houdini" and "Money from Home." For HOW THE WEST WAS WON he directed The Railroad sequence.

WHAT IS CINERAMA?

★ CINERAMA is a process of simultaneous filming by three synchronized cameras. These cameras are pointed at different angles to encompass 146 degrees of horizontal planes and 55 degrees of vertical planes. This approximates the full breadth of human vision. The films are then projected by three synchronized projectors and shown on a curved screen. ★ Today's CINERAMA is, in effect, the product of ten years of research and technological refinement. Early CINERAMA (ten years ago) had various defects such as vertical lines where film was joined, distorted figures and clumsy sound. Fred Waller's original invention has been developed into its contemporary medium by Douglas Shearer, Head of M.G.M. Research; Tom Conroy, Vice President in charge of Cinerama Production; and John Caron, Head of Cinerama Research and Engineering. Old problems have been solved with the addition of new devices until there are no longer discernible defects. ★ CINERAMA employs seven channels of stereophonic sound. There are five points of sound dispersed behind the screen. There are side speakers right and left of the audience, as well as speakers behind the audience for a "total surround" sensation. The sound system is provided for by 35 mm magnetic film which runs on an electric reproducer, which interlocks with the projectors. ★ The screen surface is a series of louvers on a curved panel. The curved screen adds a dimension and helps create the final realistic effect. ★ The color film for CINERAMA is manufactured by Technicolor and has been made by the "imbivition" process. This process insures positive registration when printing the film from the three CINERAMA cameras. It also achieves improved color matching between the three panels. ★ Extensive testing shows CINERAMA ready for a new motion picture era—an age where the audience can live a real story on the screen.

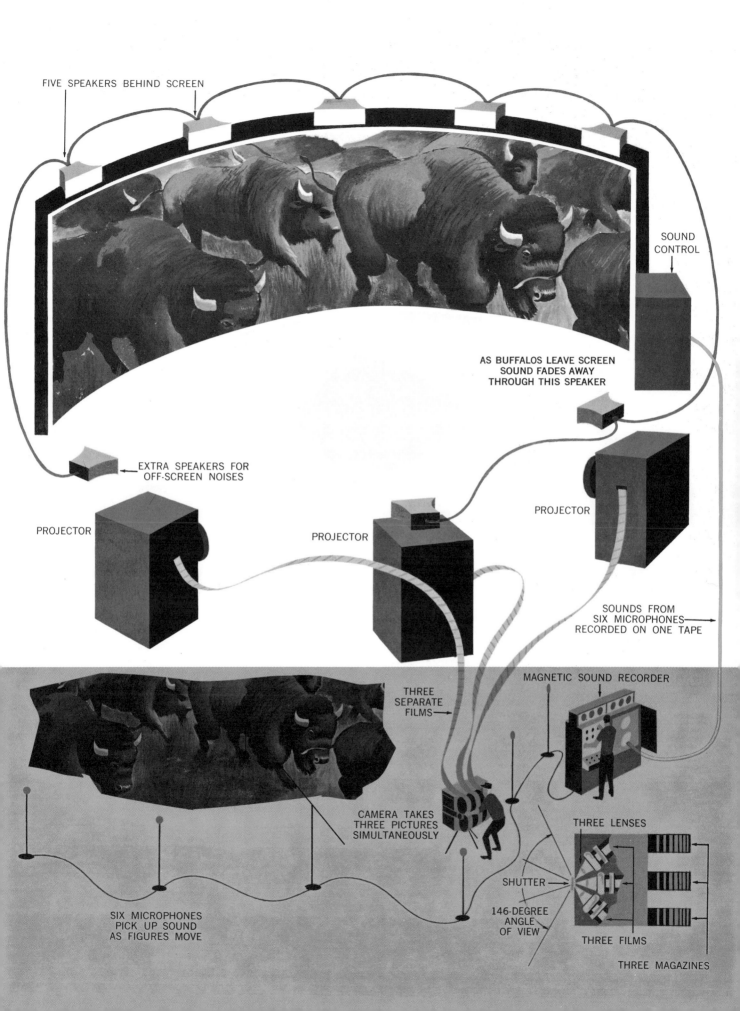

FIVE SPEAKERS BEHIND SCREEN

SOUND CONTROL

AS BUFFALOS LEAVE SCREEN SOUND FADES AWAY THROUGH THIS SPEAKER

EXTRA SPEAKERS FOR OFF-SCREEN NOISES

PROJECTOR

PROJECTOR

PROJECTOR

SOUNDS FROM SIX MICROPHONES RECORDED ON ONE TAPE

THREE SEPARATE FILMS

MAGNETIC SOUND RECORDER

CAMERA TAKES THREE PICTURES SIMULTANEOUSLY

THREE LENSES

SHUTTER

146-DEGREE ANGLE OF VIEW

THREE FILMS

THREE MAGAZINES

SIX MICROPHONES PICK UP SOUND AS FIGURES MOVE

On November 1, 1962, a London audience, including members of British Royalty, gathered at the Casino Theatre for the glittering world premiere of *How the West Was Won*.

The spectacle that was unveiled on the screen was even more overwhelming than the bejeweled audience, and time and time again applause broke in on the action.

At the conclusion, London's critics went off to seek new adjectives to describe *How the West Was Won*, predicting it would run ten years, stating it was one of the most monumental entertainments ever conceived. This reaction has taken place in other world capitals as the film has opened around the world.

Here are excerpts from those first reviews in London:

"Here is the first Cinerama feature film as distinct from spectacular for spectacle's sake. A splendiferous all-star story that might have been called *Around the West in Fifty Years*. . . . Cinerama contented itself in the early years largely with dizzy roller-coaster rides and heart-swallowing ski jumps. Now at last it has exploited the screen's wide-open spaces to the full by letting its cameras loose over the wide-open spaces of American history. . . . The dialogue is more articulate and the individual acting more emphatic than epics of this magnitude normally allow. . . . But it is the picture that tells the story, and superbly it does it, with its buffaloes stampeding into our laps, its trail of covered wagons trundling against a purple mountain skyline and its agonizing scene of rafts caught in a foaming caldron of rapids. . . ."

—The London Daily Mail

"It has a kind of surge and splendor and extravagance not to be despised."

—The London Times

"You must not miss this. . . . A wonderful slice of giant entertainment served up by three directors—John Ford, Henry Hathaway and George Marshall, and a whole host of stars who really act out the story."

—The London Daily Sketch

"Now, in *How the West Was Won,* it [Cinerama] essays, with great success, the depiction, over its massive projection depth and breadth, of an epic drama, a Western that banishes almost all other Westerns of the past into a background of comparative mediocrity. . . . This is a show that is going to run for, maybe, years to come."

—The (Jewish) Chronicle

HOW THE WEST WAS WON

"What does success sound like? At the packed preview this week of *How the West Was Won*, it sounded like *'Wheeee...'*

Which was us, the audience, letting our breath out again.

We followed it with applause that splintered round the London Casino like hand grenades.

Rush for your tickets at once. The Klondike gold strike won't be in it. Not only does the latest Cinerama film tell a story—correction, it tells a dozen stories—but it packs into them, only now as part of them, all the spectacular thrills people expect from Cinerama since it gave us our first roller-coaster ride.

We shoot crazily down the Ohio River rapids on a pioneer family's raft, and if that doesn't shake your blaséness, wait for what's to come.

We whip up the horses to get away from the Redskin tomahawks and suddenly the screen resembles six Grand Nationals being run abreast.

SPINNING

Whenever a covered wagon spills over, the Cinerama camera is right inside spinning round and round with the occupants.

We watch buffaloes stampeding down a hillside—surely, you think, a dam of treacle must have burst somewhere—and the next minute they are roaring past and all round us like ten thunderstorms.

What next? you ask, when the dust settles and you verify you haven't been left with a buffalo on your lap.

What next? A tremendous train crash as gunmen duel with lawmen on the caboose and both sides try to avoid being made into meat sandwiches by a slithering freight load that includes a ship's boiler, a steam roller and a Pharaoh's pyramid of pine logs.

No wonder we whistled our relief.

A super-epic like *How the West Was Won* does a thorough job of shucking off your sophistication. It sends you out feeling pounds lighter in heart. And amazing to relate, it makes good history as well as eye-popping hyperbole.

With Spencer Tracy as narrator, it follows the fortunes of a settler family whose chronicles include not only the landmarks of America, but the famous faces of Hollywood.

In the first episode the buxom daughter (Carroll Baker) of the family's bearded patriarch (Karl Malden) sets her cap at a beaver trapper (James Stewart) and traps *him* into stammering matrimony.

In the second, the other daughter (Debbie Reynolds) plays a high-kicker who has been left a gold mine and hitches a ride by covered wagon to California to claim it.

She survives not only the Indians, but the pursuit of the wagonmaster (Robert Preston) and a gambler (Gregory Peck), who is the kind of man who would take a bet on how many petticoats the saloon girls wear.

But Debbie is soon persuading him to chuck in a winning hand in order to win her own.

With the Civil War, the spread of the railroads and the coming of law and gun-rule to the Southwest we move into the second generation (George Peppard), but find slots for such senior citizens as John Wayne, playing General Sherman, Raymond Massey as Abe Lincoln, Richard Widmark, Eli Wallach and Henry Fonda, who is nearly unrecognizable as a hunter with handle-bar mustache and hair down to his back collar stud.

The conquest of the West is made immensely stirring by a trio of directors, John Ford, Henry Hathaway and George Marshall—veterans who can take in the immensity of the plains and at the same time as tiny but telling a thing as the wag of a dog's tail to welcome a warrior home.

And I rejoice to report another near-conquest.

It is the once-jittery Cinerama screen which now holds its three pictures almost as steady as a six-gun."

— London Evening Standard

"The first fictional Cinerama film, *How the West Was Won*, is a thundering, ear-splitting smasheroo of a spectacle. The giant screen bulges with stars, superbly colored scenery and punchy action. . . . Injuns whoop across the screen. There is a stampede of what looks like five million buffaloes. A raft is caught up in a fantastic, terrifying battle with seething rapids. Above all, there is a pulsating sequence in which Eli Wallach leads a bandits' raid on a train. This must be marked up as the biggest screen thrill since the famous chariot race in *Ben-Hur*. . . . I see no reason why this rich, sprawling, star-studded entertainment should not run for years."

— The London Daily Mirror

"The climax is the greatest train wreck ever filmed. At the end of it you could hear the escape of held-breath all over the cinema."

—The London Evening News

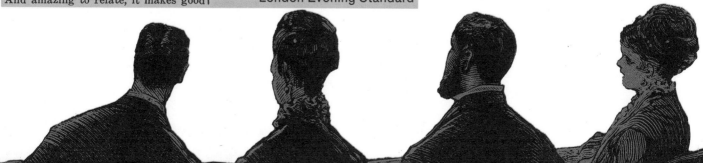

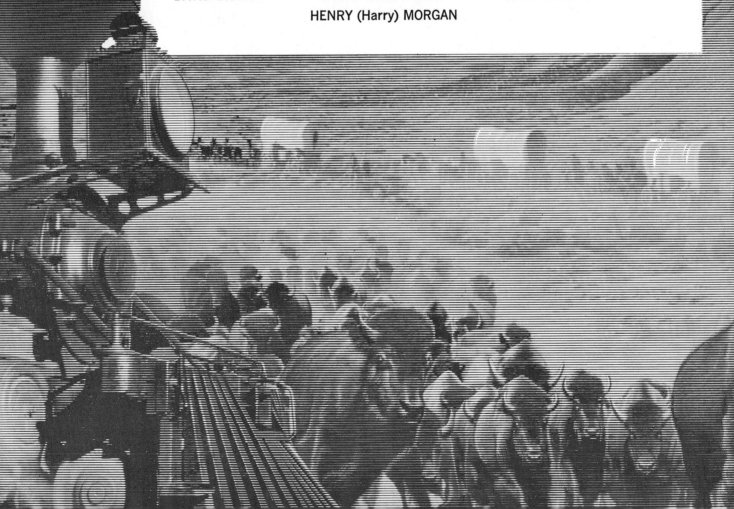

Metro-Goldwyn-Mayer & Cinerama

PRESENT

HOW THE WEST WAS WON

Starring

CARROLL BAKER	GREGORY PECK	ELI WALLACH
LEE J. COBB	GEORGE PEPPARD	JOHN WAYNE
HENRY FONDA	ROBERT PRESTON	RICHARD WIDMARK
CAROLYN JONES	DEBBIE REYNOLDS	*Narrated by*
KARL MALDEN	JAMES STEWART	SPENCER TRACY

Co-starring

BRIGID BAZLEN	ANDY DEVINE	THELMA RITTER
WALTER BRENNAN	RAYMOND MASSEY	MICKEY SHAUGHNESSY
DAVID BRIAN	AGNES MOOREHEAD	RUSS TAMBLYN
	HENRY (Harry) MORGAN	